Young Learner's

LOOK-n-LEARN

VEGETABLES, HERBS & SPICES

Vegetables

Artichoke

An artichoke is the bud of the thistle plant flower. Cooked artichokes are a rich source of antioxidants. They also aid digestion.

Asparagus

Asparagus was first grown in Greece about 2,500 years ago. It can be green, white or purple. It has many health benefits and is used in cooking.

Bamboo shoot

Bamboo is the largest member of the grass family. Bamboo shoots have been used as food in Asia for many centuries.

Bean

A bean is a pod containing seeds. There are many different types of beans like French beans, long beans, Romano beans, purple beans, etc.

Beetroot

A beetroot grows under the ground. It is deep red in colour and very healthy to eat. It is most commonly used in salads. It is also used as a natural dye.

Bok choy

Bok choy is a leafy vegetable rich in vitamins and minerals. Also known as the Chinese cabbage, it is commonly used in Chinese cuisine.

Bottle gourd

A bottle gourd comes in different shapes and varieties. It has a fleshy and soft texture. The skin is usually removed before cooking.

Broccoli

A broccoli looks like a small, dense tree with greenish-white branches. It is a member of the cabbage family. It is a rich source of vitamins C and D.

Brussels sprout

Brussels sprout belongs to the cabbage family. It is a leafy vegetable which is eaten cooked or pickled. It contains anti-cancer compounds.

Cabbage

Cabbage is one of the oldest vegetables known to man. It is a low calorie and fibre-rich vegetable. It is eaten cooked as well as raw.

Capsicum

A capsicum may be green, yellow, orange or red in colour. It is also called bell pepper. It has many small seeds inside.

Carrot

A carrot is either red or orange in colour. It is a good source of vitamin A, minerals, etc. It grows under the ground. Its most commonly eaten part is the root.

Cauliflower

A cauliflower looks like broccoli, but is white in colour. It grows from a seed. It looks like a flower but is actually a bunch of tiny stems.

Celery

Celery is a green, stick-like stem with saw-like leaves. Its leaves are used in salads and its seeds are used as spice. The stalk is usually cooked.

Cucumber

A cucumber is long and green in colour with many small seeds. It has about 96% water content. It is a rich source of vitamins, calcium, folate, etc.

Eggplant

An eggplant may be purple, green or white in colour. It has a smooth skin and many small seeds inside it. It is also known as aubergine.

Fennel

Fennel has yellow flowers and feathery leaves. It is used in cooking as well as medicine. It is a good source of dietary fibre.

Fenugreek

Fenugreek is widely used in cooking. Dried or fresh leaves are used as herb and seeds are used as spice. It has useful medicinal properties.

Galangal

Galangal looks like ginger but has a more potent flavour. It has several health benefits due to its antibacterial properties.

Garlic

Garlic has a strong pungent flavour and hence is also known as the stinking rose. It is widely used in cooking as well as medicine.

Ginger

Ginger is an underground stem. It has a strong aroma. It is used as a spice and herb around the world. It is also used in dried and powdered form.

Leek

Leek is a cylindrical vegetable with long broad leaves and a white bulb at the base. It is eaten raw as well as cooked. It is very rich in antioxidants.

Lettuce

Lettuce is a green leafy vegetable which is mostly eaten raw in salads. It is a rich source of many minerals and nutrients.

Onion

An onion is a vegetable with a strong flavour. It is available in many varieties. It is a good source of manganese. It is eaten raw, cooked and even pickled.

Parsnip

A parsnip is a cream-coloured root vegetable. It is related to carrot and parsley. It is commonly used in stews and broths, and is very nutritious.

Pea

Peas are contained within a pod. They are round and green in colour. They have a sweet taste and smooth texture. They are high in sugar content.

Potato

Potatoes have brown skin, but are white or yellow on the inside. They can be eaten boiled, fried or baked and are used in a variety of dishes.

Pumpkin

A pumpkin has a hard shell, but is soft and smooth on the inside. It is orange in colour. It is a rich source of vitamins and antioxidants. Its seeds are also edible.

Radish

A radish is a white-coloured vegetable. It has a slightly pungent taste. It is a root vegetable. It is a very good source of vitamin C.

Soya bean

Soya bean is an oilseed used to make oil, soya sauce, soya milk, tofu, etc. It is a rich source of plant protein. It is the only vegetable that contains complete protein.

Spinach

Spinach is a green leafy vegetable. It is a rich source of iron, vitamins and many other minerals. It can be eaten raw or cooked.

Sweetcorn

Sweetcorn grows on a cob and is one of the most widely grown vegetables. It can be eaten raw, boiled, roasted, canned, etc.

Sweet potato

A sweet potato is a starchy root vegetable with a sweet taste. It is a rich source of iron, other minerals and vitamins. It is also high in beta-carotene.

Turnip

A turnip is purple from the outside, and white inside. It is a root vegetable. Roots and leaves of the turnip are edible.

Yam

A yam has a rough skin that is difficult to peel. The skin can be pink or light brown. Its flesh is white in colour. There are about 600 species of yam.

Zucchini

Zucchini is a squash which can be dark or light green in colour and can grow up to a metre in length. It can be eaten cooked or raw.

Herbs

Basil

Basil is a leafy herb used to add flavour to dishes. It has a strong, pungent yet sweet smell. It is also used for its medicinal properties.

Borage

Borage usually has blue flowers. It is also known as star flower. It is used both fresh and dried. Its flowers have a sweet honey-like taste.

Chives

Chives are long thin leaves with edible purple flowers. It is used as a spice or seasoning while cooking. It is a member of the onion family.

Coriander

Coriander is an aromatic herb used to add flavour to dishes. Its leaves are used in cooking and for garnishing. It is one of the most widely-used herbs.

Dill

Dill has feathery green leaves. It has small yellow and white flowers. It is used fresh as well as dried. Its seeds can also be used.

Lavender

Lavender bears purple-coloured flowers. It is used to make oil, perfume and as a flavouring agent for food. It was also used in mummification in ancient Egypt.

Lemongrass

Lemongrass has a lemon flavour. It can be used dried or fresh. It is commonly used in making soups, curries and tea. It is also known for its medicinal properties.

Marjoram

Marjoram has green fragrant leaves. It is used as a herb as well as to make essential oil. It helps to ease coughs and colds and relieve indigestion.

Mint

Mint has a fruity, aromatic taste. It is used in tea and as a flavouring agent in many dishes and sauces. Its essential oil is used in perfume, candies, cosmetics, etc.

Oregano

Oregano has a strong stimulating taste. It is an aromatic herb widely used in cooking and making medicines. It has antibacterial properties.

Parsley

Parsley is a bright green, leafy and fragrant herb. It is commonly used in soups, stews, salads and for garnishing. It is very rich in antioxidants.

Rosemary

Rosemary has a sweet flavour. It is a woody plant with fragrant, needle-like leaves. It is also called anthos. It is a member of the mint family.

Sage

Sage has soft leaves that are grey-green in colour. It is used to add flavour to food while cooking. It is also used as a herbal remedy to cure many ailments.

Tarragon

Tarragon has glossy green leaves. It is an aromatic herb used in cooking. It usually grows in dry places. It is also used as a traditional remedy to stimulate appetite.

Thyme

Thyme is an aromatic shrub with a pungent flavour. Though the flavour is better when fresh, it can be used dried too. It has health-promoting properties.

Turmeric

Turmeric is widely used in cooking to add colour and flavour. It is also used as a dye and for medicinal purposes. It is known as the golden spice of India.

Spices

Cardamom

Cardamom has a thin skin. It has small black fragrant seeds inside. It is used in cooking and for flavouring tea and coffee.

Cinnamon

Cinnamon has a strong flavour and is used in making desserts and savoury foods. It is used in a stick as well as powdered form.

Clove

Clove is a fragrant flower bud. It is used in cooking as well as medicine. Its oil is beneficial in reducing toothache. It is also useful in treating common cold.

Cumin

Cumin is a dried seed. It is used as a flavouring agent in many dishes. It is also eaten to aid digestion. Roasted cumin seeds have a strong aroma.

Paprika

Paprika is a spice made from capsicum. It is used to add flavour and colour to rice, stews and soups.

Pepper

Pepper has a strong pungent flavour and a sharp taste. It is used as a spice and seasoning in almost all cuisines.

Saffron

Saffron is the world's most expensive spice. Its threads are used to impart colour and flavour to many dishes including desserts.

Star anise

Star anise is used as flavouring for many dishes. It is also used in tea for medicinal purposes and as a digestive aid.